A Book of Poems

Release the Winged Ones

By

Sarah Whiteley

Published by 2nd Tier Publishing
Wimberley, Texas, USA
© 2015 All rights reserved

First published by Sarah Whiteley
© 2013 All rights reserved

Book design by Nikos Rovakis
Editing by Niamh Carey
Cover Art by Jeraldene Lovell-Cole
Author Photo by Shiila Safer

Whiteley, Sarah
Release the Winged Ones

ISBN: 978-0-9862290-5-3

Life-Force billows like a kite in flight
Heart's tremor skips a beat
How may the Journey unfold?
Will Life fly me? I hear…YES!

From Release the Winged Ones

ACKNOWLEDGMENTS

If I thanked all the Beings within this Creation
I would start right from Life's Source
And end with Infinity

Yet between these environs, Dear Ones gifted presence
Passion, generosity
Pure energy, deep heart

So please meet the Beauties who poured forth their magic
I deeply thank each One
For gifting their Gift

Thank you Maria, for co-journeying this Lifetime, with wholeness as our guide, for celebrating the unfurling of wings as new landscapes beckon, and for tending the hearth's heart to burn even stronger.

Thank you Vanessa, for journeying another year of wholeness, and for bearing witnessing to the tender transformations, forever willing to offer a inspiring word and a reassuring hand.

Thank you Nikos, for creating such beauty with your graphic artistry and Hosting with such heart, presence and ease.

Thank you Niamh, for animating the poems with such gracious, grammatical precision and for exploring the deeper patterns of the manuscript with your heart and soul.

Thank you Jeraldene, for tracking and reflecting back the power held within poetry as it unfolded, and for expressing the essence of this creation with your elegant artwork.

Thank you Kamyar, for offering your calmness and IT wizardry to create such a rich web-container for the Book to bathe in.

Thank you to my family, Jonathan, Ann, Mark and Ginia, for your love, presence and gentle holding.

INTRODUCTION

'Release the Winged Ones'
Chronicles a Pathway
Of
Living Wholeness
And
Conscious Evolution

One Pathway of Life
Lived in 2012
and
Informed by the
Individual and Collective,
Visible and Invisible,
Breadth and Depth.

THE JOURNEY

In following the pathway of these poems, I invite you on a journey spanning the timeline of one year, where the gifts of experience, emotion and energy are recognised, worked with and learned from in order to inspire our next level of growth and conscious evolution.

Dare you step into the fire of your heart's song? This poem marks the beginning of the journey as we step onto the pathway in the depths of Winter. At Awakening we are asked to make the first of many difficult decisions, a request emphasised in Parallels where the reality of the options and the possible consequences become visible.

Once we make our decision, we need to create the space for change to happen and we meet the beauty of possibility in Growing Pains. Yet there is also pain in change and letting go of old forms. We confront this in Pains Meet. One way of dealing with this pain is to seek help from the wise, as in Pythia and in If I Stood There Could I Stand the Standing where we face our truth. Blossom shows us another way to meet pain: we must break apart old boundaries and thought forms in order to open the space for change. In the cycle of the year, we move from Winter into Spring and step Towards the Unknown ending with the question 'who am I now?'

Love's Life Crucified takes us to Easter and we see how tradition, ritual and community teaches us something about 'who we are now'. Through these insights we hear Nightingale Echoes and feel the gifts of renewal and re-birth. We move into Early Summer with Kalo Mina, heralding the first of the month of May and we explore Brushstrokes of Hope and shadows in Soul Conversations to support our exploration of transition. We begin to see the need for temperance and balance in Transition's Heart Skips a Beat, the equal balance of darkness and light as we move towards Mid-Summer. In rebalancing, we challenge our small selves and small lives in Re-Calibration: the greatest gift we can offer our world is to be our full selves.

A second major transition meets us as we embrace Pre-Flight's Soft Gaze and the pain of manifesting our full self-expression – our Soul's Calling. Chariot-like, we take to the air and ask what now arises as the space is opened with the gifts of Truth the Messenger? We embrace the quest and expansion, whilst asking how to allow space for healing, tracking back and forth and connecting with our ancestors in Healing Across Aeons.

We explore new ways of seeing and referencing who we are now and where we might go and, through this, we Anchor in the Waters and open a new level of understanding as we Release the Winged Ones, inviting healing and reaping the reward from seeds we have sown. Yet this is an exhausting process and, needing to tend the inner, more vulnerable aspects rising, we withdraw to give space to our inner hermit in All-One-Ness. Having taken the time to reflect and listen inwardly, we then ask, how do we now move onwards in Elegance's Step and where are we best placed to offer service?

Being Reclaimed by Homeland signals another shift point. Reaching home at Mid-summer at the Solstice Peak we ask what we might learn from the invisible and the metaphors of the year as they rise in parallel with the Mid-summer sun? We ask for guidance in Awaiting Orders at Dawn and travel through Pathways of Grace in order to Re-Turn Towards Unity. This difficult process of reuniting what has been suppressed

– through being willing to live wholeness at every level in our lives - requires courage. And so we find ourselves Moving Over the Edge, taking a quantum leap from where we were before, Leave Taking towards the new. We see The Bigger Picture and we begin to sense what it is we wish to say Yes to.

True Voice is awakened, and the grace of being willing to give ourselves fully into the journey. We slowly enter into Autumn, Awakening to Death and allowing the cycles of life to move towards completion. The Spiral Turns and we embody our understanding of our place in life's cycle, and we continue to negotiate the challenges of learning how to navigate our next steps when the old reference points are no longer there. We receive new insight on how life has transformed through North Star Re-Positioned and are reminded of how asking the right questions can support our new navigation. In The Power of the Flower Reading we dive deeper and gain more insights, using our intuition to surface our deepest knowing, until, finally reaching Wit's End, we face that which no longer serves, acknowledging this in order to enable its release.

If I Cannot Live in Peace is the result of asking our heart our most burning questions and, through acting with courage, we begin to release our deepest patterns in Shame's Shame Forgiven. In doing this Soul work individually, we sense we are also releasing patterns of the collective. We surface the Echo of the Original Cut, and reveal the deep wounds that require healing in ourselves, our countries and cultures and the need to reconnect with the past in order to do this. We take up The Sacred Sword and acknowledge our call for truth, clarity and justice and step further along the path. As we do so, Emptiness returns: we need to keep releasing old patterns, including those that challenge us most. We see that Ambiguity and other invisible aspects hold both challenges and gifts, and we invite The Birthing of new ways of being that are not possible without risk and not-knowing. This connects us with the endearing Truth of Love that invites every human heart to risk, knowing that the courage to love is immense and deep within us. We see The Evolving Thread weaving and how life is moving us deeper into uncharted territory, yet the pathway is clear and open. We allow the Embrace of the known and the unknown to sit together, until reaching The Gateway and the moment of transition to the next phase of life, including the longing for Union - of life, love and wholeness - and the willingness to release the waiting, the longing and the emptiness.

With the next pathway beginning to emerge on the horizon, clarity and truth are with us and we initiate the Sacred Sword Re-Set to orientate our steps with steadiness as we continue to release the barriers and chains that hold us back. Finally, we see that we have travelled the journey with our Heart and Soul and to our surprise, we find ourselves entering Uncharted Tracks where life and the next new pathway beckons once more.

INDEX

Dare You Step Into the Fire of Your Heart's Song?	1
Awakening	3
Parallels	4
Growing Pains	6
Pains Meet	7
Pythia	9
If I Stood There, Could I Stand the Standing?	10
Blossom	12
Towards the Unknown	13
Love's Life Crucified	14
Nightingale Echoes	16
Kalo Mina	17
Brushstrokes of Hope	18
Soul Conversations	19
Transition's Heart Skips a Beat	20
Re-Calibration	21
Pre-Flight's Soft Gaze	22
Truth the Messenger	24
Healing Across Aeons	26
Anchor in the Waters	28
Release the Winged Ones	30
All-One-Ness	31
Elegance's Step	32
Reclaimed by Homeland	34
The Solstice Peak	35
Awaiting Orders at Dawn	36

Pathways of Grace	40
Re-Turn towards Unity	42
Moving Over the Edge	44
Leave-Taking	47
The Bigger Picture	48
'Yes!'	49
True Voice	51
Awakening to Death	52
The Spiral Turns	53
North Star Re-Positioned	54
The Power of the Flower Reading	55
Wit's End	57
If I Cannot Live Peace	59
Shame's Shame Forgiven	60
Echo of the Original Cut	62
The Sacred Sword	64
Emptiness	66
Ambiguity	69
The Birthing	70
Truth of Love	72
The Evolving Thread	74
Embrace	77
The Gateway	78
Union	79
Sacred Sword Re-Set	80
Uncharted Tracks	85

Dare You Step
Into the Fire of Your Heart's Song?

Bridging now and then
Holding
All that is still to be
And has become
The Song
Sung with heart-full breath
Beyond the Self
Blessings' wealth

How Life wishes for trueness
For newness
While Time turns its face
To meet Love

Dare You Step
Into the Fire of your Heart's Song?
Sung loud
Into night's sky
Brilliant stars
Shining patterns
Mapped across Aeons' face

Lighting shrouded places
Lost in the mist
Thought to be
Gone for good

Bridging then and now
How Time turns
To face a New so true
So blue in skies
That dance
Towards the horizons
Beckoning You

To trace the Tides
That turn and yearn
Until You see what's true
For You, for Now

Not judged as better
But shelter
For the tides
To rise and fall
That call the ships
To return to shore
Nestled, settled
Until the dawn awakens

And beckons You
Once again
To venture
Into Bright Adventure

Awakening

You reach inside
And touch
Love

How magnificent
To know you
wait

Amidst the movement
Into Being

Threads collide
Like Lightening
Resonance

The Breath
Of New Life
Releases

Parallels

Parallels running along the edges of Time
Travelling between the shores of the new World
And this one being transmuted
How will we transit?
By Swimming, or Sinking?
The latter, if un-committing.
Come, the edge IS crumbling
What will WE choose?

Parallels running along the edges of Truth
Travelling between the shores of the new World
And this one being bridged
How will we tender?
By Loving, or Fearing?
The latter, if uncaring.
Come, the edge IS wavering
What will WE choose?

Parallels running along the edges of Trust
Travelling between the shores of the new World
And this one being trampled
How will we relate?
By Honouring, or Mis-Deeding?
The latter, if non-believing.
Come, the edge IS cracking
What will WE choose?

Parallels running along the edges of Beauty
Travelling between the shores of the new World
And this one being neglected
How will we attend?

By Creating, or Negating?
The latter, if non-cultivating.
Come, the edge is captivating
What will WE choose?

Parallels running along the edges of Hope
Travelling between the shores of the new World
And this one being dreamed
How will we participate?
Joyfully, or Wantonly?
The latter, if not wholeheartedly.
Come, the edge is beckoning
What will WE choose?

Growing Pains

Remember
As a child
When bones ached
And sinews stretched
Elongated in form
Opening more space
For life to move
Freely

And now
Stretched again
In zones and tones
Of a psyche
Growing in patterns
Breathing more space
For life to move
Freely

Pains Meet

Pains sat at the airport
Coffee cups balanced in hand
Swirling-shapes
Painted on curve's surface
Of the breathing place

Right Timing named NOW
And Time stood still
Awaiting Silence
Pains' tender voice spoke
Truth's Grace awoke

Pain turned to face Pain
Deep Grief-lines etched
Stretched across landscapes
Weary from the escapes
Of journeys wide

Staying strong for so long
Had cut a groove
Into the heart-beat
That craved a new start
For a sacred part

Why had Pain not seen
Pain's vulnerability
At the gifting bridge
Seeking shores
That nurtured the Soul?

Pain was shocked
Wired close to the bone
That one touch shook
Life's entire globe
And broke every bulb

Charged with Knowing
That Consciousness held
Tight in her embrace
Until Maturity said YES
To Reality's Grace

Pains' static waves
Panic-stricken thoughts
Marched too and fro
Forever on the go
Then Exhaustion said

'No, Enough!
Let go
Tend the slow
Burn of
Loss
And flow'

Pythia

Pythia

I am You

You are Me

Born not Born

Aeons Old

Sacred Told

Between the Cracks

If I Stood There,
Could I Stand the Standing?

May I pray at the Step
On which you stood for Aeons?
For Ages
For Moments
For all Time

If I stood there,
Could I stand the Standing?
What would I see?
What would I believe
And know?

To throw forward
A lifeline from the Future
To the Culture
That awaits
The turning of the Tides

Would I have the Courage
To name
What is flowing
From the depths
Of the Centre,

From the Belly of it All
That flows
In formations

To seed and breathe
New Life?

The seeds that ripen
Amongst the grass
And are threshed
In time
When all is seemingly lost

And yet
This is the Birthing
Of the New
The true flow
Rising unabated

Translated
Into the Soul-Fullness
Of the actors
The benefactors
That pass on

The Passion
That is
No longer theirs
But theirs
To share

Blossom

Space Blossomed in the Springtime

Cascades of Colour

Showers of Shiva

Towards the Unknown

Towards the Unknown

I turn

And bow

Who am I Now?

Who

Will I Become?

In time

No time

Now

Love's Life Crucified

One Journey moved the People
Into timely confluence
Come closer now, stay awhile
Time to love the reason hence

Wheels spin and come to resting
Moving hearts beating bright
Step forth inside the Gateway
The bell's still silent night

Candles bright held in a circle
Water at their feet
One lifetime moved the people
To rest in Heart's Retreat

Rows of reverent subjects
Psalms quietly stir the Soul
Moving towards the night air
Greetings bless the inward flow

Spirit rides the waves of heart-song
Flowing into cup-u-lets
Still the bells hang patient
Waiting to toll world's debt

Crucified Life's bold starlight
A Body of Consciousness
Procession calls us forward
To journey and seek the Quest

Arms linked and candles blinking
Light-beams weaving forth
Wind's breath blows the Light out
Light again, with Loving Truth

Frogs croak the river chorus
Hosting our journey-way
Until we meet the Bridging
Pause to sing this day

Night-time sees sea air waving
Breaking lightly on the edge
Rounding road and moving homeward
Candlelight's honoured pledge

Stooping below Death's framework
Awash with blossom-rain
Song, prayer and Gospel's music
Breathing out the pain

Hope is quietly waiting
Sensing when it is time
A day of rest and listening
Consciousness aligned

Flower gifts of friendship
Hope-signs' potency
Peace and quiet reflection
Invites to parea, come see

Blessèd drawn to witness
Love's Life Crucified
Hope in Trust and Will-full
To rise and rise and Rise

Nightingale Echoes

Nightingale echoes at Distance
Far on the edge of all Time
Birthing the migration of Movement
Calling Life's Centre to Shine

Darkness itself bridges Starlight
Bugs blaze in criss-cross Lifelines
Candlelight flickers night's Love-trails
Tracing earth-curvature Rhymes

Blissful is Night's deepest Silence
Humanity sleeps in their Beds
Trust is Re-Woven in Owl-space
Love casts her net in thick Threads

Sea speaks her sound across Time-zones
Arching her voice up the Path
Aegean-Sea magic breaks Shoreline
Life's greatest-gift Aftermath

The Past is now present in Newness
The New is Re-Written through Birth
Life speaks night-time's soft Chorus
Nightingale echoes gently: be Love

Kalo Mina

Earth shimmers with Light

Nested in cycles of receding Moon Beams

Brilliance arises from the Edge

Tones of grey echo Distant Lands

Brushstrokes of Hope

The Ground is shaken

Newness curves the Circle-arc

Broad brushstrokes of Hope

Till the parched ground

Soul Conversations

Arising from the depths of Knowing

Soul breathes traces of a Hidden Language

Blossoming wonderment awakens

Untraceable lines reveal the Shadow's song

Transition's Heart Skips a Beat

Space breathes in Time
Transition's Heart Skips a Beat
Plum red toes rove the tiles
Treading lightly towards the Future

Chronos Re-Members Cycles
Kairos expands the Birthing Field
Seeds' knowing scatters Hope
Wide, in all directions

Horizon beckons Dusk
To rest on Subtle Line's edge
The Threshold draws day's end
Shadows lengthen into darkness

Silence opens the Void
Love tracing Dragonfly wings
Transforming Fires breathe
Calling forth Hope and Magic

Parea and Community
Pave Re-Patterning's Grace
Right Timing calls for Movement
Paintbrushes' weaving waves

Space breathes in Time
Transition's Heart Skips a Beat
Plum red toes rove the tiles
Treading lightly towards the Future

Re-Calibration

Re-Calibration through the liberation
Of all that no longer serves

The Curves rising strong
From the portal of it all

Fall into the zones that hone
The edges of Life lived too small

Call for Truth to smooth the metal
Into a sword that Soul can hold

Bold

Bright

Cast forth

Into the Fire

Of Rebirth

Pre-Flight's Soft Gaze

Sun kissed the Tears
That fell on Shore's Lap

Baptismal blessings
For a Love in Transformation

Heart hung heavy
As lungs heaved with Right Timing

Rhyming the release
Toward New Life just beyond

Sun stroked translucent wings
Awakening from soft shells

Radiant Tones shimmering
As the breeze brushed them dry

Veins stretched like tree-branches
Taught with Soul's knowing

Flexed in preparation
For Pre-Flight's soft gaze

Pathways morphed wildly
With options now gifted

Hands stretched breathtaking
Expressions of Life to take hold

Pulses raced as choices morphed
Into bifurcated distinction

Wings flexed with deep knowing
The trajectory now set

Truth the Messenger

How far is my Land from your Land?
Should I land closer?
And hold my Land against yours?

Blessèd tensions
Blend shorelines
Unseen to the eye
Yet felt at Depth

Bridging Expansiveness
Truth the Messenger
Hope the Message

How far is my Edge from your Edge?
Should I edge closer?
And hold my Edge against yours?

Blessèd tensions
Blend chasms
Unseen to the eye
Yet felt at Depth

Bridging Courageousness
Truth the Messenger
Hope the Message

How far is my Love from your Love?
Should I love closer?
And hold my Love against yours?

Blessèd tensions
Blend brilliance
Unseen to the eye
Yet felt at Depth

Bridging Breathlessness
Truth the Messenger
Hope the Message

Healing Across Aeons

Across miles
Across timezones
Across timelines
Across Aeons

We Heal

The disconnects
The massacres
The torn
The tormented

We Turn

Weaving threads
Laced with Love
Sisterhood healing
With glittering hearts

We Burn

Breaking open
Tender tensions
Spilling forth
Life's Blessings

We Grieve

Tear-banks burst
Aeons' treasures released
Natures cleansing
Sacred Ritual

We Witness

Cleansed, we prepare
Emboldened, we pack
Heartened, we leave
Soon we arrive

We Weave

Across miles
Across timezones
Across timelines
Across Aeons

Anchor in the Waters

Anchor in the Waters
Raise wombs of fluidity
Grace's Perpetual Embrace
Curve Sounding's Potency

Birth Evolution's pooling
Nurture rising tides
Doula Movements' Magic
Create boldly, energize

Write rites for deepest passage
Hold Oceans' Earthly Love
Antidote Confusion
Caress Pain's birthing dove

Blend tender-time Beginnings
Stream dreams in all you care
Spin threads in sweeping wake-trails
Sculpt Souls Extraordinaire

Touch timeless shifting canyons
Earth's indelible watermarks
Etch pathways friends may follow
Modelling the sparks

Erase idle frequent seeing
With a swiftly blinking eye
Reshape the shifting shorelines
Amplify flying high

Watch Tsunamis arch the Fault Lines
Tremble tremors across the Grooves
Revere seascape power-lessons
Soak Destruction's moves

Call Planetary Communion
Re-Union Life's divide
Heal death sores, birth the newness
Awaken Soul's deep cries

Whisper dreams with Starlight
Quench drought-taut heartened-shells
Water bodies bright and blue-toned
Flow forth with blissful Spells

Whitewash the World with Beauty
Crescendo Blessing's Tone
Be ready for Life's Echo
Welcome Living Wholeness Home

Release the Winged Ones

Awakening to a sun-soaked Earth
Butterflies grace the airwaves
Wings dusted with gifts of home
The Birth Place of the Soul

Life-Force billows like a kite in flight
Heart's tremor skips a beat
How may the Journey unfold?
Will Life fly me? I hear…YES!

Reap seeds sown these years
Nature's cyclical reciprocal service
Verdant within Fertile Ground
Awakening with Abundance

It's time for Gratitude to breathe
And Release the Winged Ones
Brimming with Goodness
Filled with stories and Hope

Awakened by Life's Vibrancy
Anchored in Humility
Standing with Dignity
Lush with Potency

Until the moment of flight
Trust approaches with Patience
Witness of Sacred Beginnings
And whispers 'It's Time'.

All-One-Ness

Beings Part
A pattern lived
With a Soul
For Earth's Longing

The Heart's Song
Beating strong
Heightened awareness
Climbing, chiming stairs

As footsteps grace
The solitary space
The Hermit's
Birth Place

Arriving and leaving
Only one place
The Space of Aloneness
All-One-Ness

Elegance's Step

Standing on the Edge of the Chasm
Mouth wide
Edges gaping
Depth unknown
Will we fly?
Hit the floor?
How will we know?
Until Elegance Steps

In Trust
Full thrust
We Call the Winds of Change
To guide wide-wings
With Ease
And glide Life's Gracious
Flight-paths high
Beyond ground impact

Yet Gravity calls Downward's Motion
Slow locomotion
Into the forward stepping
Towards the unknown
Zone of the future

Breath catches
Snatching straws
From crystalline laws
Held beyond the claws
Of happenstance

Saying 'It's NOW OR NEVER!'
Staying sheltered does not serve the
Winged Ones
Ours is the Expansive Journey
With Gravitas
Hourglass turns
Life's Commitment beats
Bifurcations' Heart
Towards New Horizons

Standing now on Safety's Edge
The Known World
Nestles close with Trust and utters
'Fly - all will unfold
In accordance with the True Tone
Elegance's Step is now wide open
Stream forth
With Higher Consciousness'

Reclaimed by Homeland

You are Home

The Stones said
Bones awakened
To the resonant
Ring-tone

Chiming down
The Spine
Into a Chord
Of Union

What do you want of me?
Now your Soul Soars

What do you ask of me?
Now my Step Falls

What do you expect of me?
Now my Voice Calls

What do you need of me?
Now that Destiny Draws

Soul Awakens
Steps Shaken
Voice Crescendo
Destiny Echoes

The Solstice Peak

Solstice breathed raindrops' misty morn
Tongue-tied from dampness, his reed moist
Unable to vibrate with the precise Tone
Present on a summers' day

And yet, Solstice knew the Tone to strike
Irrespective of the downward rush
Embracing Raincloud's message:

'Be Well
Be True
Be the Bridge to the New

Light the Worlds that emanate
In the direction of Consciousness' tender touch

Live with Grace
Allow the pace
Of Guidance to pave the Way

Bring Joy and brush against the faces of All

Call forth Resonance and Presence
Unity incandescent
Wholeness' Moon-Crescent

Boldness
And
Truth'

Awaiting Orders at Dawn

Is it true that we are groundless?
The Place that housed our growth-path
No longer clear
And the Prism-Shift
Kicking any sense of Safety into touch
That clutching
The same straws
Hold not one ounce of Gravity

Is it also true that flight from this nest
Is the next Big Test?
Being invited to rest into
To edge
Beyond the Line of Safety
And free-fall
Into the Call
Of dancing airwaves

Life's Beating Heart
Catching
Snatching
Rasping
Rising gasping from the throat
As the Known disappears
Into the distance

Yet what is the message
Held within the tightness?
What shout
What tone

What cry
What moan
Wants to fly into space
Beyond the deafening Dead Zone?

What screams
Release the dreams
Cowering beyond the screens
Of Knowing's imposing
Dress code?
What icons
Release the Aeons
Caught in the bygones
Within Love's
Broken World-Views?

What images
Release the sweetness
Fluttering hearts' beatèd-ness
Into newness
Still unfolding?

What traces
Release the crazes
Of Rage's Red-Phases
Breaking free
Into Peacefulness?

The curl will unfurl
Within the swirl

Of Right Timing
Rising high on the tide
Testing Anchor's Grip
Stretching Lifelines' Whit
Stilling Grief's long Whip
Lashing Truth to the Hip

Awaiting Orders at Dawn
Gracious Blessing's
Broad brushstroke
Weaving Coherence
Beyond the Shadow's Grave
Until the phoenix form
Crowns the rising dawn
Beyond Destruction's Holy War

And in Time
Peace weaves
Golden threads
Within deep tears shed
Until blue skies
Ease beyond
The clouds
Of Life's Darkest Night

Pathways of Grace

Stop idly conversing
Blind busyness coercing
Hold space for Truth's Birthing
Walk Pathways of Grace

Breathe space within oceans
Bridge bravely 'cross notions
Crave breadth and depth motions
Spread Beauty with Words

Create Change that Reveres
Birth stared-stratospheres
Weave Consciousness' Light-Years
Through each moment lived

Curb the urge to converge
Release Wisdom's Soul Surge
Align movements to merge
Set Pace to Unfurl

Arch the arc of the back
Touch DNA's Time Track
Witness Power's Deepest Map
In Life's Beating Heart

Walk Bold-Steps' Immensity
Stand tall with Tenacity
Hold space for Life's Sanctity
Call forth the New Path

This sacred preparation
Is the task for the taking
Great Turning's Creating
The Pathway of Grace

Re-Turn Towards Unity

She sat with Confusion
Tears offering Diffusion
Wondering why it was so
difficult
To ask Masculine for help

She saw Him reflected
Somewhat disconnected
Untuned and untrained
In His Seeing and Speech

Truth's Touch avoided
Soul's Knowing now Voided
Both fearing the force
Of Love's Deepest Heart

Feminine's Deep Need
Was for Union In-Deed
For Wisdom's Re-Balancing
And Wholeness in Pact

The Crack in this plight
Called for Feminine's Invite
'Let's Re-Turn towards Unity
Dear Masculine, this Way'

Re-Quest now said 'Stop!
Let Life-Pretence drop
In service of Wholeness
And Destiny's New Step'

So here lay Her Clue
In Re-Seeding tears' hue
Re-Shape and Create
Deep Openings for Two

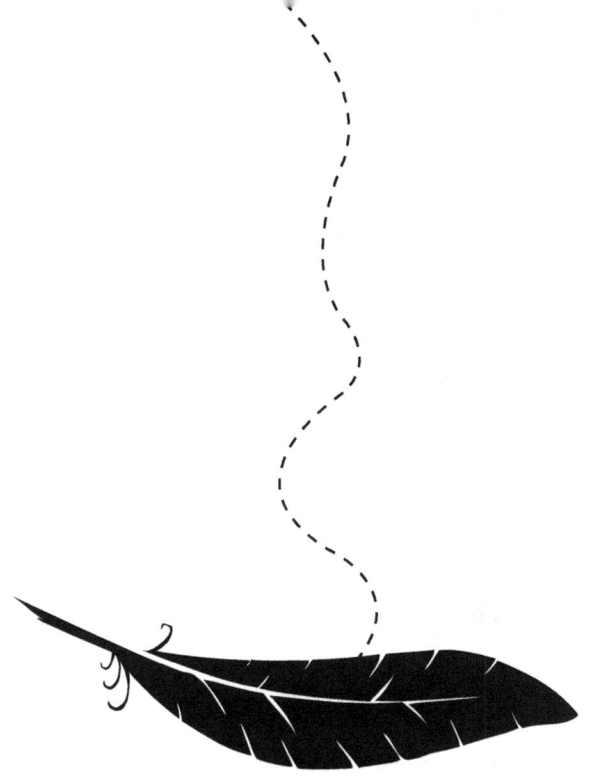

Moving Over the Edge

Last night I was called up!
By The Office
Issuing my next Destiny-Line
To step into my Power
Now is the hour
To do
What I have come
Here to do

My work is Calling
The pathway still unclear
But emerging so I may be
Ready to let go
Of memory lines
and timelines lived
And now being released

Like an abseiler
Moving backwards
Towards the Edge
Taking a stance that feels
Counter-balanced
Utterly terrifying
As the Edge
Looms closer

And yet
To slowly trust the rope
The positioning
The movement

Is actually the way to go
With Presence
And Patience
And Trust

I am also the belayer
Holding the rope
For my Soul-Self
The one moving
To stand on the Edge
In the newness
With all that is ME

The rope is me too!
An aspect so strong
And resilient
Able to hold the tension
Of the movement
Within and beyond
The line of sight
Beyond flight

And so the time comes
When returning
To safety's ledge
Creates more uncertainty
And ungrounded-ness
To create more ground
And strength
I must say YES!

Time to traverse
The Edge with Commitment
At this point

Of NO return
To Transition beyond
Requires precision
Absolute trust in Self,
Newness and Life

Re-Orienting in movement
Is Artfulness' Navigation
Knowing that the onward journey
Is exhilarating
Yet the new ground
Is vertical
And the angle rejigged
Real and secure
My route is now taking me
In descent and beyond
This Journey
And Calling
To integrate and bring
Another level of Wholeness
And Expression
Of Soul-Self

So I say 'thank you'
Say 'YES'
To the movement in motion
Opening hands and heart wide
Embracing it all
Let the rope hold
The Vertical Edge
To Ground and Soul Self

Leave-Taking

Standing on the runway
Engines burning in readiness
Time to take flight
Into the New World

The Old World echoes
Tugging at the heart
Calling Memory's Field
To honour the transition

Yet Memory's Field
Has erased itself
Shedding skin that
Took up Sacred Space

How the heart aches
Tuned into pastures new
Known receding fast
Unknown still awaiting

Time will tell which way
This way, or that
Questions abound
What is Life Becoming?

The Bigger Picture

What is the Bigger Picture?
Do we dare name it?

What is our piece to hold
That frames the new path-
ways?

It's too big for one to see
Like the Elephant Game
Touching the tail, the leg
The trunk

Yet, it's all ONE
And yet the blessèd begin-
ning
Is to the hear the bell toll
That touches the Soul

And pulls the Timeline
Closer to the Heart
Knowing that Courage is
stretched
99.5% in Trust, 5% still
trembling

The Art is to come together
To share the Edge
Of the Line's touch
Knowing Horizons are
beyond the Seen

Call forth the Seed
That trembles to the touch
Earth the Planet's Pulse
And Birth the Homeland

That has been pushed beyond
The Heartland's Knowing
Where Trust is just
Beyond the seen

Call forth the Call
That awaits Humanity's All

The True Tone that blesses
Creators' Truth

'Yes!'

Have you ever said 'Yes!'
To this level of YES?
Do you even know
What this YES represents?

How will you,
Until you open the portal
And step
With a bold step

And say, 'well, actually, Yes!'
Otherwise 'Maybe'
Is held in the heart
And 'Yes' remains
Untouched, unrelated
Unrequited, apart

A 'Yes' means a step
Towards
That which is sought
A wholehearted thought
And a sweep of the sword

A compromising
Wavering 'Yes'
Will not do
Not to step resoundingly
Into this NEW

This 'Yes'
This bold, untamed,
Unashamed 'Yes'
Is the Threshold
That opens Truth's veils

This is the Step-Through

To throw Life wide open
To receive the Bright Light
Of the Numinous World
And embrace the Deep Shadows
Residing there too

Both exist side-by-side
Perhaps that's why we resist
But to be kissed
By this 'Yes'
IS the blessèd unrest

It sends the 'No' skyward
And 'Maybe' to retreat
It appears YES
It is time
To say a deep 'Yes'
To YOU

True Voice

Sinking into the lush garden
Sounds echoing overhead

The time for diving has arrived
Silence descends once again

How best to travel
The Fine Lines of Destiny

Woven in magic strands
Within your womb-like pages

Listen with precision to Intuition's True Voice

Know the Subtle Tones
Create mass Transformation

Intuition's Voice rises
Guiding Millennia's Knowing

Re-Membering to Creators'
Sacred Stepping Stones

Standing now at the Threshold
Earthed feet stretching deep

Soul's roots quake wildly
As Intuition's Voice sings

Awakening to Death

He arrived once again
Breathing deeply into every cell
Rankness offering no solace
Within my aching heart

His cycle was persistent
As the setting Sun
And the falling leaves
In Autumnal bloom

He seeks the place of Pain,
Loss and Grief
The tempered place between
Now and the Future

He left no stone unturned
Never letting go of Awakening
What needs to Die?
Witness the letting GO

The Spiral Turns

The Spiral Turns
As Next Step is taken
New realities shaken
Into submission

With the decision
Of creating movements
Uttered
Aeons ago

The Time Ticks
As Next Step is taken
Yearning towards
Unknown landscapes

Knowing Death
Sits quietly in the shadows
Rearranging everything

The New Opens
As Next Step is taken
Hands masking
Eyes from a world

That catches breath
And makes little sense
But is
SO clear

North Star Re-Positioned

I saw the Re-Alignment
Framed boldly in the skies
I stared with pure amazement
Burning Truth before my eyes

North Star WAS Re-Positioned
No longer where I knew
Re-Aligned within the Matrix
Balanced amidst the New

Starlight had profoundly shifted
Night skies landscape Re-Framed
Brilliance shown in new forms
Re-Grouped, but not Re-Named

Striking cords beyond all doubting
Wild patterns all anew
Newness HERE and Sky-shaped
Truth's birthright, through and through

Why had it taken so long
For me to see the Shift?
Perhaps it made sense real-time
Within Galactic's Worldly Gift

The Power of the Flower Reading

The Power of the Flower
Ignited Soul to Awaken
And explore
The core question
With Loves' Deepest Heart

Guided, transcribed
Insights flowed side-wide
Spinning
From Pattern
To Wisdoms' Still Word

Truth's Magic opened
Mind's Wandering Re-Woven
Heart's
Worthy Knowing
Blessèd eye that can SEE

Amidst all the swirls
A Pathway unfurled
Signposts
Now beckoning
Life-Stepping Stones of Truth

The heart of the read
Was 'Release the Keys' Seed'
To trusted
Companions
Bless hearts with Strong Will

Watch out for the spin
They no longer win!
It's Curl
And E-x-p-a-n-s-i-o-n
That serves the Next Phase

Bridge New Timeline's Gaze
Present-Future-Phase
Weave strands
Already moving
Right into the mix

It no longer aids
To chop wood in spades
My dear
Time to soar
And Release the Ace Wave

Wit's End

This day was heralded
By Wit's End and Death

Drawing a line across the heart
Saying 'D'ya mean it?'

'YES!' I cry,
'Enough!
Enough!
ENOUGH!

If I cannot Live Peace
I don't want to LIVE.'

Death asks again
'D'ya mean it, my LOVE?'

'YES!
Enough!
Enough!
ENOUGH!'

Life's Thread weaves forward
Defined over time

Drifting through landscapes
Where daybreak breathed peace

It's time to listen
To the Tides of Truth

Pulsing from The Source
Into uplifted palms

And Live Peace

If I Cannot Live Peace

If I cannot Live Peace
I don't want to live

Wit's End uttered
Towards Silence

Death rode the depth
Shuddered-breath and wept

Dead-Beat as lungs
Heaved full stretch

Peace pleaded with Soul
'You need to awaken!'

Death's Pulse raced
Towards Silence

Hearts beat in time
Knowing Passion's decline

Until Soul-Friends gathered
Showering Pain with Love

The wall around the Weary Heart
Unveiled Shroud's Curve with Light

Shame's Shame Forgiven

Shame threw off his cover
That shrouded his Presence
Throwing Secretive Mystique-ness
High into the air

Shackles broke at nightfall
Once again at break of dawn
Delusions scattered skyward
Shattering Worlds' View

Shards cut deep
Voice quaked and rasping
His presence now unanchored
Voice curved and black

Beyond all Knowing
His frailty was releasing
Layered Pain for lifetimes
Dust-dreams of dew

Right Timing called forward
Shame's cross of the river
'Release Life Blamed-silence
It no longer serves Joy'

Shame bowed in reverence
Raise now the DAM WALL
Release Misery's Distortions
Into blissful beam-showers

It was time to release
Blame's Patterns of Torture
Crushing deep Joy-filled toning
Into Heart-fire's strong song

Forgiveness stepped forward
Witnessed Shame's Shame forbidden
Breathed Love's Light completeness
Into his Courageous Soul

'You, my Dear,' she uttered,
'Are a Precious Soul Guardian
Who protected the Sacred
Within Subtle-stone hardship

Bless you, my Dear One,
You've held Tension Deeply
It's time to release Life
Into the bright light of day'

Echo of the Original Cut

Race-Memory Ascended
Soul's Aching Backbone
The time is now here, dears,
To echo the song

Re-Weave Native Culture
Re-Member Place-People
Re-Contract with Forgiveness
To heal the Original Cut

Truth was so banished
On levels so widespread,
From Knowing, from Hope,
From Unity, Home

'When WAS this?' Aeon asked
Race-Memory listened
Echoing Tones rising within
Truth's Beating Heart

Wisdom's Peace lay
Deep in the Lines-Ley
Etched across Sacred Faces
Before ONE polarised

Yet ears of the Resonant
Lay gently on Earth's cheek
Tracing the Echo
To the Original Cut

Transcend Incoherence
Within inner planes' seeing
Into the near World
Saying, 'I witness you HERE!'

Wavelengths curved wildly
To Wholeness' Beat
Truth's Pulse-rate quickened
Rhyming with Joy

Amnesia peeled backwards
Unwrapping Assumptions
Within Myths' Mundane-entity
Aligning Life's Soul Tone

Listen to Soul's Octave
Source the light radiance
Revel in the glory
Grace-filled Grand Scale

Time to weave Bliss'
Now-ness with Memory
Embed within Earth's Core
From Indigenous Root

The Sacred Sword

Threaded lines tremble through Time
Struck within Night-times' Wakefulness
Hilltops curve the Horizon's Sultry
Form
Beckoning the listening at depth

Voices echo below the Splintered History
Abbey dissolved at Faith's Tide-Turning
Greed, mistrust, a weak-willed king
Blind-witness of the Sacred Prayer

How did the Monastery maintain Grace?
Stones and prayer beads lost yet not forgotten
Remnants left in numbered recognition
Reverent witnesses and idle observation

Yet within the Landscape, treasure remains
Hidden at depth in tunnelled enclaves
Awakened Guardians patrolling broken
walls
Seeking hands and hearts of the Trusted

Engrave Blessèd Beginnings within the
Eight-Eight-Eight
Torn by kingly orders within Fifteen-
Thirty-Nine
Yet within the Sacred Settlement's nave
The pristine Sword of Truth remains

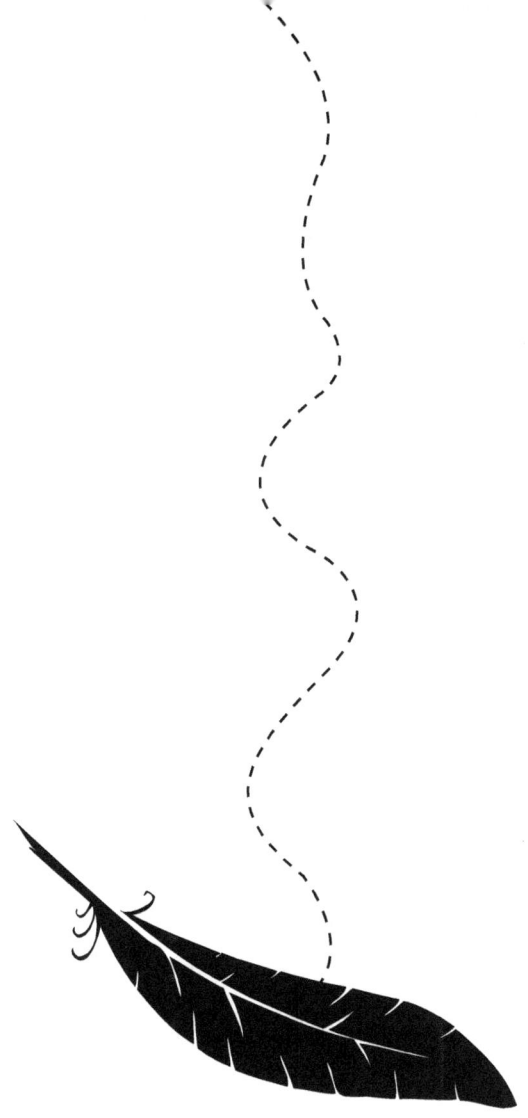

Emptiness

Between the Waves
Of Ebb
And Flow
A space lies empty
A place
Forgotten
Until the Tides
Released Her Gifts

Treasures
So pure
So present
Utterly iridescent
Omnipresent
Incandescent
To the rise and fall
Between the waves

Beneath the over-laps
Is Emptiness
Resting gently
Breathtakingly lamenting
Within the space
Of the still
Moving
Alone-ness

She beckons
And listens
Weaving pathways
Into All-One's deepest Heart
Emptiness stands with Pain
Holding the frame
Of Not-Knowing's Tears
With Knowing's Fears

Time to resist the desire
To fill Emptiness' mouth
With words
Time to listen
To Her Wisdom
Resting, blessing
Life's pure gold

To face the Graceful Self
Required stature
Trusting the sacred structure
Of Emptiness' hand
Willing to weave
Gossamer threads
Across Graciousness' Void
Dignity rising forth

Hers was the touch
Of Sacredness' birth
Stretched
W-I-D-E OPEN
Revealing the tides

Within inner and outer
Dimming the clatter
Of a distant drone

Soon, rounded edges
Of all that was needed
To shelter in the storm
Rose to meet the dawn
With those knelt
At Emptiness' Altar
Without words
Faltering no more

Staring into space
Quelled the tidal race
Allowing Love's Touch
To abide
Emptiness' Gift
Allowed Souls seeking shift
To weave the next wave
Along Life's Shoreline

Ambiguity

Who are You,
Ambiguity?
One that rests
In the in-between

        Holder of Paradox
        Anchor
        Of half-truths,
        Truth-holder nonetheless

Feared by many
Loved my some
Touched by Tones
Of spectacular spectrum

        Birthplace of Knowing
        Resting in the cracks
        Weaving light threads
        Of Sacred Wisdom

Tender of Timing
Not to be rushed
Caller of Nuance
Prismed with Beauty

The Birthing

What was Birthed here?
In the space of the Unknown
Where the tides rose
Amidst the rocky outcrops
And crossed the mid-point
To where the grass grows

It came out of the Blue
Where the glue peeled away
From the Non-Truth
And yielded to its Truth Partner
Witnessed from between the Cracks
Shining like the morning Sun

The Circle birthed the Voice,
The choice that called Crisis
To 'Name its Stand'
Arising, born and dawning
The space for the New World
Naked, within the open palm,

Europe opened her Glistening Eye
Having held her Seeing cloaked,
Closed for far too long
Mystics and Elders blessed Circle's Pledge
Curving the Edges engraved
Within Soul's Weaving Work

Partnership Breathed Deep
Within the creaking's sweep
Calling the Dawning of Time's
Hand to tick in a different rhyme
It's open, dear friends,
Europe birthed its New Home

Truth of Love

Love's Presence resonated
With a power
So True
So Pure
So utterly sure
That it broke through
Sounds that no longer
Rang true

It touched Soul to Soul
Transforming the mould
That contained Life's
Journey to date
Transforming Life's Blindness
Blood's Silence
To rush through
With Grace

Heart's quickening beat
Had been struck
With a Tone
Birthed with Soul Fire
Breathing essential Love

What happens to the Witness?
When the Truth is palpable
It breaks us open
It calls our hearts
To reveal the Cracks
And opens the Portal
To the next Level
Of Depth

The Evolving Thread

Life throws
The Line forward
Or is it US?
In partnership
With Life
As Soul Friend
Co-Crafting
The New Trend

Who defines the Voice?
Beyond Separation-Choice
As the Trajectory
Appears so clear
And aligned
With Source
That the Truth
Cannot be denied

While the Line travelled
Bends against the strain
The Pain of ending
A time
Now complete
Where some contracts retreat
To the file marked
'Closed'

And the Evolving Thread
Shines new Light
So bright

Into the contracts opening
Crafted with Awakened Love
Making hearts quiver
With the shivering beauty
Of the Rising Dawn

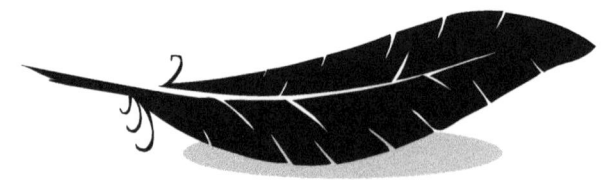

Embrace

What does the Bear say?
As Life nestles close
In the warm embrace

The cold echoes
Through the corridors
Of the heart, tested to the End

Endurance bridges the divide
Cultures shift
Listening at distance

As the slow shock
Of the Gentle Heart
Rises from the ashes

The Gateway

Waiting at the Gateway
Wheels of light spin
Creating waves
Bright bathed days
Within the true
Blue yonder

Time to ponder
The World just beyond
The line of sight
Paved with In-Sight
Touched with overdue

Silhouettes rise
Amidst the cries
Of Life saying:
'It's time to step
Beyond Regret
And into the New'

Dare we trust
The Soul's Thrust
Stretching far
Within starlight's
Watchful gaze?

Dare we open
And caress
Time's broken
Longing for Wholeness
With Bold Steps?

Union

Tears rise
Flooding sight
With the Truth
That Love is sought

Gone are the days
Of waiting
For Life to shine
Through the Heart

Gaze rises
And journeys to the place
Where Two Cups rest
Against each other

Leaves dance
Entwined
Yet separate
On the mirrored surface

Patient, waiting
For flow to cascade
Across open lips
Filling Longing with Bliss

It's time to manifest
The Love Line
And call Soul's Twin
Also seeking its other

Wholeness gasps
As Emptiness is quenched
And Love's
Container overflows

For Love has arisen
Within Soul's Longing
And called the Blessèd
Sacred Union

Time to Journey forth
Sharing blessings bright
In noonday sunlight
Longing's Quest complete

Sacred Sword Re-Set

With purposeful step
Triad moves within Sacred's Walk
Casting forth a Weaving Thread
Dancing to its own accord
Only to find
The Gateway chained

Tracks Re-Turn
And Viewpoint beckons
Crowned with Obelisk's
Tender stance
Yet
Direction remains illusive
Entry cloaked with Disorientation

The advice is heard:
'Move away from Interference
Create the airborne lemniscates weave
Then the compass will reset

Allow the Sensing Steps
To point Truth's Direction
Where Bygone's words
Calm the speaking

Mark the place with stones
Of the Sacred Turning
To Anchor the Burning Threshold
On Spider's Lofty Loom'

Words scale out
The Compass resets
Crowns cascade
The pavement steps

Until a weary traveller
Turned towards home
Glances the Movement's Edge
Ignited by Life-times' Crash

Written by spinning wheels
Trembling the Heart's
Weakened Pulse
Diverting daylight's intention

In an instant
Pathways Reconfigure

The Confluence complete
The Sacred replete

Until

The Next Phase
And Authority steps across
The metallic threshold
Toward empty halls

Caverns creak
Under Heart's Bleakness
Ringing hard against
Silence's Listening ear

And Sensuousness wills
Austere to lessen
Its grip and listen
To the Emptiness within

And unravel its hold
Release Chains' Grip
Beyond tightness
Towards the Reign of Hope

Glowing Wholeness
Rings True
And turns the ground
From Past's Shallow Grave

Time to Re-Instate
The Sacred Ritual
And the chain
Refraining Celebration

To release the Wellspring
Stopped in its tracks
Disallowed from flow
From shallow's powered paths

The Gateway is breached
And the Subtle Waters
Rest on the pillows
Of Passion's Pledge

Bubbling from the yard
Across the shard
Guarded too tight
In the scabbard

The Flow's faintness
Echo's across life's greatness
And spins the yard's eye
Glistening with longing

So gossamer fingertips
Catch the beaded flow
Touching the Heart's Knowing
That release is near

And with purposeful step
And musicians' surprising jet
Streams the energy
From well to hilltop

Unity Re-Sets
Rising high in Eve's mist
Beckoning the birthing
Of a brighter day

Tributary's flow
Unchains the Gates'
Impenetrable reign
And, swings open

The Sacred Touch
Breaches the Stand's Banks
And opens the flood gates
Of the Sacred Past

Aeons' Parched Layers
Breathe in the soaked Earth
And forgive History's
Discreditable acts

Past is replenished
Not banished
But healed
Its Courageous Heart

Uncharted Tracks

Flooded Lines
Delay movement
Slow the Pulse
Shift the Track
To new trajectories
Not once,
Not twice,
But thrice.

'Futures, please!'
Life speaks.
'Newness is our Timeline
Curving the Journey Plan
Time-span
To create a
Destination Trans-Script
Mind-Shift.

Pay attention,
Slow Down.
Let the wheels
Move freely,
Release the
Feelings
Of drag.'

Now
The doors are sliding

Gliding
Guiding
A New Path

Different
Yet
Waiting,
Captivating
The next rhyme

Stay awake.
Life's Symbols
Are weaving
Tapestries
Now breathing
New realities
Into the Dreaming

Where Past
Is heard
Yet
Mute

Transmuted
Into
The Pulse
Arising
Beyond
The din
Of
Distraction

Now
Attraction

Leads the Edge
Releasing the Ache
Laying wait
In the Creation Game

Time to board
The train
And travel
Along
Breathtaking
Uncharted
Tracks

www.ingramcontent.com/pod-product-compliance
Lightning Source LLC
Chambersburg PA
CBHW061453040426
42450CB00007B/1339